SPEAK TO THE WIND...
IT SHALL OBEY!

SPEAK TO THE WIND... IT SHALL OBEY!

The Believer's Authority Over The Weather

Pastor Renard Farrior

Scrivalo

a division of Illuminated Paths Publishing, Inc.

www.ipathsinc.com

Copyright © 2018 Renard Farrior
ISBN 978-0-98425-069-1

All rights reserved.
Written permission must be secured from the publisher and author to use or reproduce any part of this book. No portion of this publication may be reproduced, stored in a retrieval system, or transmitted in any form or by any means – electronic, mechanical, photocopy, recording, or any other – except for brief quotations in printed reviews, without the prior permission of the publisher and/or author.

Unless otherwise noted, all Scripture is taken from the *King James Version of the Holy Bible.*

The Holy Bible: The Amplified Bible. 1987. La Habra, CA: The Lockman Foundation.

The New Testament for Everyone (NTE). Scripture quotations are copyright © Nicholas Thomas Wright 2011.

Contemporary English Version (CEV)
Copyright © 1995 by American Bible Society

Published by

Scrivalo

a division of Illuminated Paths Publishing, Inc.
P.O. Box 94568 Birmingham, Alabama 35220 USA

Printed in the United States of America

ACKNOWLEDGEMENTS

- **I would like to thank my lovely wife, Sonya:**
  Your encouragement and support in life and ministry is immeasurable in value and more appreciated than I could ever express.

- **To my sons- RJ and Reshad**:
  Thank you for supporting daddy.

- **To my father, my mother, and my mother-in-love:**
  I honor you and appreciate you for supporting me as I grew as a man, husband, father and Minister of the Gospel.

- **To my Coaches, Pastors, and Spiritual Teachers:**

  I want you to know just how much you are appreciated. If I had to stand in front of each of you and tell you how I feel about you, the pressure of leaving something out would be risky. So, I salute the three of you here in this God-inspired book.

  - **Reverend Jackson** (Mt. Olive Baptist Church)

    Even though Rev. Jackson has gone on to be with the Lord, somehow I know he will get the message. Thank you!

  - **Pastor Steve Green** (More Than Conquerors Faith Church)

    My second coach, Pastor and Teacher- Thank you!

  - **Dr. Michael D. Moore** (Faith Chapel Christian Center)

    My third coach, Pastor and Teacher- Thank you!

CONTENTS

INTRODUCTION

CREATION NEEDS OUR HELP

1 Creation Has An Attitude   11
2 Creation Is Backsliding   19
3 Creation Is Having Labor Pains   29

BEHIND THE CURTAIN

4 The Temperature   41
5 The Weatherlies   47
6 Territorial Authority   59

THE KEYS OF AUTHORITY

7 The Power Of Agreement   75
8 The Believer's Weather Forecast   85
9 Speak To The Wind   93

INTRODUCTION

I started the journey of writing this book because it is an assignment from God. In the beginning, the work of writing included much hurt, pain and sadness within me. Not because some terrible weather-related event had impacted me personally. It was pain and heartache caused by the images of destruction and devastation I would see on the television in some far away state or the images I would drive by in my own city. The hurt and loss caused by what the world calls "natural disasters" is not from nature at all. I knew that! But, I wondered, *how many others don't know it.*

These disasters have changed the lives of millions of people all around the world. In many cases, people have lost all of their worldly possessions and financial security- homes, cars, jobs. Even more devastating is the loss of countless lives. So many of you reading this book right now have personally experienced the pain and suffering that so-called *"natural disasters"* have left behind.

But, just like everything else we deal with on a regular basis, severe weather has become "normal" to us. We just take the safety precautions we have been trained to follow and we just accept it.

Well, my assignment is to write this book and tell you, IT IS NOT NORMAL and you should not JUST ACCEPT IT! God has given you AUTHORITY and POWER OVER IT! That's right! I am telling you that God has given His born-again, Spirit-filled children authority and power over all of creation, including the natural elements that cause severe weather events and so-called "natural disasters".

Let's begin with 2 truths:

1. **Natural Disasters-** There is nothing **NATURE**-AL about the weather-related events we call natural disasters. **NATURE** has no God-given right or assignment to cause disasters. More than that, nature does not want to be a part of causing disasters.

2. **Severe Weather-** is simply an atmospheric event caused by a combination of natural elements that come together to kill, steal and destroy. The natural elements of wind and liquid or frozen water *(in the form of rain or snow)* were created by God to be a blessing to man.

I know there may be some ridicule that comes with the assignment to write this book, but I have never asked God, *"Why me?"* I am prepared for the warfare of my assignment to address this area of life, so *why not me?*

I understand that for many in the Body of Christ, the premise of this book is a totally new way of looking at our authority as Believers. For others, it's not new... *you've heard that we have this authority*... but you just don't understand it. Then, there are others for whom all of this is just plain foolishness.

Regardless of where you are in your understanding and acceptance of the Believer's authority over the weather, my hope is that you will walk with me through this new territory of dominion and power. It's not new territory because we didn't have this authority before now. No, man has always had dominion over creation.

It is new territory in the sense that this generation is allowing God to enlarge and expand the borders of our understanding to effectively walk in this authority.

This is not just a book that I have chosen to write. This is a Kingdom assignment to declare war on the enemy who has unlawfully taken control of the earth's atmosphere and the elements that God created. The enemy is using God's creation to cause weather events that are severe, dangerous and too often deadly.

Part of my assignment is to prepare the children of the Most High God for the battles we will face in exercising dominion in our individual territories of family, home, and possessions. Another part of my assignment is to prepare God's family in our collective responsibility to exercise dominion in the territories of neighborhood, city, county, state and nation. Then, there is that part of my assignment that requires me to dive even deeper into God to prepare myself and the Body of Christ to take dominion and possess the larger territory of the whole creation, which is the responsibility of the **manifested sons** of God.

My heart's desire is to share the revelations that God has given me about the Believer's authority over the weather. Just like the woman on the front cover, I want to pull back the curtain on these severe weather events and show Believers that we have dominion to command the elements and dispossess wicked spirits of their power to use God's creation against mankind.

I want to do my part to equip you with knowledge from God's Word that I pray will light a fire in your heart and fan the flames of your faith to believe that when you

**SPEAK TO THE WIND…
IT SHALL OBEY!!!**

CREATION

NEEDS

OUR

HELP

CREATION HAS AN ATTITUDE!!!

1

SPEAK TO THE WIND... IT SHALL OBEY!

Severe Weather and Weather Disasters come in several different categories: *tornadoes, hurricanes, strong winds, earthquakes, tsunamis, floods and lightning strikes.* Every Kingdom principle of authority and dominion that I explore with you in this book applies to all of these categories. There is no **dis-order** or **dis-ease** in creation that is not under the dominion of God's Word and under the dominion of the man/woman decreeing that Word. With that said, I will focus on tornadoes to explain the Believer's authority over all severe weather events.

Why tornadoes? Because most of my dominion experience has been gained in exercising Kingdom authority to subdue tornadoes. The part of the world I live in is the inland, south-eastern region of the United States. On average, we experience over 400 tornadoes per year. That's about one-third of the 1200+ tornadoes recorded annually for the entire United States. My home state of

Alabama experiences nearly 50 tornadoes each year and is ranked 7th in the number of tornadoes recorded annually for each of the 50 states.

As I was writing this book, my wife and son reminded me of something that made me LOL. They reminded me that I have a long relationship with tornadoes. A relationship that began in my teenage years. Can you guess what my high school's mascot was? Yep, the Tornadoes.

I can't tell you how many pep rallies and game night cheers and chants I heard with my ears and spoke out of my mouth that were… *in some way shape or form…* expounding the awesomeness and power of the MIGHTY TORNADOES.

Isn't it funny how God has a way of bringing together things we may only see as coincidental. My early exposure to the "might" of tornadoes created a confidence down in my soul that all of the bravado about these twisting winds was true. As I began to understand my Kingdom authority over them, my mind had to be renewed not to see them as a symbol of school spirit and pride. But rather, as a curse operating against God's creation. From my perspective as a teenager in high school, anything that gets in the way of this twisting wind will be destroyed. The opposing sports team didn't stand a chance against the mighty tornadoes.

Now, I understand that the wind twisting and turning out of control is out of character. It's like the wind suddenly picks up a bad attitude. You know, like a teenager that suddenly gets an attitude and needs his parent to straighten him out.

Well, the truth is that nature really doesn't have an attitude, the enemy is just making it look that way. The natural elements really don't want to be part of the destruction. It is the enemy that works to twists everything that God created to bless, but the sons of God have the responsibility and authority to straighten it all out.

Wickedness is simply the result of twisting what God created for good; satan has no ability to create.

For example: God created music, sex and words to bless humanity, but how much pre-marital sex (fornication) and extra-marital sex (adultery) does today's music encourage and promote? God's original purpose for music has been perverted through words (lyrics) that twists God's purpose and order for the sexual experience. Scripture gives us clear examples of music being used both for good and music being used to lead people into sin.
(2 Chronicles 5:13; 7:6 and Daniel 3:5-15).

In the same way the words in today's music has been twisted to pervert God's purpose for it, so has the wind. In the case of tornadoes, this is a literal twisting of a natural element. The wind was designed to bless in the form of a soft, pleasant breeze or to help usher in the change of seasons.

In the case of words, this is a twisting of the truth. One clear example of words being used to twist the truth is how insurance companies categorize tornadoes with the words "ACT OF GOD." And, what do we- *the children of God-* do about it? Nothing! We go right along with it. We have gotten comfortable using words that don't line up with Heaven's perspective.

Wind twisting out of control and destroying everything in its path, is not an act of God. When God sends a whirlwind, it's a blessing. God sent a whirlwind to transport Elijah from Earth to Heaven. Elijah wasn't killed by the twisting wind and nothing around him was destroyed (2 Kings 2:11).

SPEAK TO THE WIND... IT SHALL OBEY!

It is time that we take our rightful place of dominion and authority as God's sons and daughters and straighten out the disorder in our Father's creation.

CREATION IS BACKSLIDING!!!

SPEAK TO THE WIND... IT SHALL OBEY!

The first time I remember really having a spiritual anger with how the elements were behaving was in 2005 during Hurricane Katrina. The first real action I took against severe weather was a combination of a little bit of an angry, rebellious attitude mixed with bold faith in God's Word.

All of that devastation and loss of life was happening in New Orleans and it made me both sad and angry at the same time. I did not have the revelation I have now about my authority over the weather, but something just didn't sit right with me about the enormous catastrophe the wind and the water were causing. So, I did what I knew to do, which was to pray for the people and help in the natural ways we could.

While the storm and flooding were ravaging New Orleans, Birmingham had a few days of very strong wind gusts or back winds from that storm. At some point in all

SPEAK TO THE WIND... IT SHALL OBEY!

of that, my attitude became rebellious against the instructions of the weather man to take steps to protect ourselves from the possibility of falling trees and power lines. One day, I decided to remind myself and the devil that God's Word instructs me not to fear. So, as an act of faith while the wind was blowing stuff around and knocking stuff down, I decided to go out into my yard and lay in the hammock. I stayed out there for quite a while, refusing to be afraid that the wind would blow anything down that would hurt me and my family or damage our home or cars.

Well, the good news is: I wasn't hurt, my family was protected and our property wasn't damaged. The bad news is: I did nothing to provide protection and coverage for anyone else because I did not know how. The elements were misbehaving all around me, but I didn't know how to stop them. In fact, I didn't know that I could stop them. That kind of misbehavior by the natural elements is a clear picture of how nature is backsliding.

Let's compare the state of creation before sin entered the earth's atmosphere and after the first man sinned. Before sin- the ground, the seas, climate, food, nature, the winds and mankind were all in harmony. Everything worked together to complement and assist the other parts. No part of creation was working against the other parts. Unfortunately, that is no longer the reality.

After sin, a large part of creation is working against its leader- *man*. Sin entered the earth and the curse by sin. In the same way the sin of just one party can disrupt the harmony and cause separation in a marriage, family or friendship, man's sin has disrupted the harmonious relationship we have with the rest of creation. Man's dominion and authority (being made in the image and likeness of God) is what sets us above the rest of creation.

However, because of sin, we are now separated from what makes us special and this separation has caused all kinds of confusion.

Genesis chapter 1 says that everything God made was good. Nothing that was made by God was bad. However, now- because of sin, the whole creation is crying out for help because the enemy is using creation... against its will... to bring harm to the earth and to its master- *man*.

It is not just the wind that is backsliding. We see the whole creation backsliding, more and more, into a deeper state of dis-order and dis-ease. Just look at the waters; they are roaring and raging and overflowing their boundaries. Earthquakes are killing people from one side of the earth to the other. Think about 2017. There were a number of record breaking, weather-related disasters that caused loss of life, devastation to property and hundreds of billions of dollars in financial burdens on governments, businesses and individuals to clean up and rebuild those areas where hurricanes, flooding and earthquakes caused great destruction.

Proverbs 8:29 (Amplified) tells us that God *"...set for the sea its boundary so that the waters would not transgress [the boundaries set by] His command..."*

Yet, the seas (representing all great bodies of water) are routinely transgressing the boundaries their Creator set for them. That's backsliding... steadily moving beyond specified boundaries; steadily moving backwards and away from the purpose and activities that have been established as proper or ideal; behavior that is out of order.

When these natural elements damage property, injure and kill people or become destructive in any way, they are **out of order**.

SPEAK TO THE WIND... IT SHALL OBEY!

WIND as *hurricanes and tornados*- out of order!

LIQUID WATER coming down as *rain* to the point of flooding- out of order!

FROZEN WATER coming down as *hail* punching dents and holes in everything upon which it lands- out of order!

Again, these natural elements have no God-given right or assignment to create severe weather events or dangerous weather conditions.

Stress in this area is at an all-time high. Just the mention of a possible storm or some other severe weather event is challenging for some. Fear and even panic grip the hearts and minds of so many. Oh, but God!

God is Faithful! God is Amazing! God is Love!

Hebrews 4:15 Amplified says,

"For we do not have a High Priest who is unable to understand and sympathize and have a shared feeling with our weakness and infirmities and liability to the assaults of temptation."

In short, Jesus feels our pain. Just knowing He understands what I'm going through and is able to feel what I'm feeling brings me great comfort. I believe His compassion is passed on to us (Believers) to feel each other's pain.

The aches I felt in my heart in those early days of learning and growing in this revelation were not just for the people affected by the weather. It was also for the people who could have done something about it and didn't know it- the Body of Christ. My brothers and sisters in Christ have the authority to do something about it, but too many of us don't know it.

Everything we see is a result of something we do not see. Jesus- as the son of man and as the Son of God (which all born-again Believers are both), showed us how to exercise our authority as it relates to the natural elements and the weather. Creation needs our help and it is time that we take our rightful place as the leader and master of God's creation and pull it back from the ever-increasing slide into decay and destruction.

CREATION IS HAVING LABOR PAINS!!!

Nothing just happens in this world. Everything has a reason even if we cannot totally understand it. There is always cause and effect, even if we can't see it. For example, the human body has thousands of blood vessels... veins, arteries and capillaries. They provide blood to every area of the body. I am not a doctor or scientist, but I am confident in saying that medical science does not have an accurate count of how many blood vessels we have in our bodies. I am also confident in saying, there is a need for each one.

When an area of your body is being attacked, you can tell something is wrong. You will experience some physical sign (symptom) like pain, numbness, weakness, fever, etc. It doesn't matter what the symptom is, its purpose is to alert you to the hidden dis-order and dis-ease in your body. These symptoms present themselves to make you consciously aware that something behind the scenes is not functioning properly; something is out of order. In the same way, God's creation presents symptoms of dis-order and dis-ease. We call it severe weather and natural disasters, but the Bible calls it creation's labor pains. You may be asking, why in the world is creation having labor pains? The answer to that question can be found in Romans 8:19-22 (KJV):

> *19 For the earnest expectation of the creature waiteth for the manifestation of the sons of God.*
>
> *20 For the creature was made subject to vanity, not willingly, but by reason of him who hath subjected the same in hope,*
>
> *21 Because the creature itself also shall be delivered from the bondage of corruption into the glorious liberty of the children of God.*
>
> *22 For we know that the whole creation groaneth and travaileth in pain together until now.*

To gain the most from this book, we must have a line-by-line understanding of Romans 8:19-22. The foundational premise of this book is that man has authority over God's whole creation *(creation is referred to as "the creature" here in Romans 8)*. To help us gain better insight into this passage of Scripture, let's do a parallel reading with the King James Version and a modern translation of the Bible that can be found online called the **NTE** (New Testament for Everyone):

SPEAK TO THE WIND... IT SHALL OBEY!

KJV	NTE
¹⁹ For the earnest expectation of the creature waiteth for the manifestation of the sons of God.	¹⁹ Yes: creation itself is on tiptoe with expectation, eagerly awaiting the moment when God's children will be revealed.
²⁰ For the creature was made subject to vanity, not willingly, but by reason of him who hath subjected the same in hope,	²⁰ Creation, you see, was subjected to pointless futility, not of its own volition, but because of the one who placed it in this subjection, in the hope
²¹ Because the creature itself also shall be delivered from the bondage of corruption into the glorious liberty of the children of God.	²¹ that creation itself would be freed from its slavery to decay, to enjoy the freedom that comes when God's children are glorified.
²² For we know that the whole creation groaneth and travaileth in pain together until now.	²² Let me explain. We know that the entire creation is groaning together, and going through labour pains together, up until the present time.

So, let's answer the question:

Why is creation having labor pains?

Creation is having labor pains because it wants to be delivered from the bondage of corruption. Creation is tired of being a slave to the decay, disorder and dis-ease brought upon it by man's sin.

One challenge we face in exercising our authority is that God's creature (creation) is cursed and corrupted. So, to further help us build our understanding of this corruption and our authority to straighten it out, let's go back to the beginning.

The first place in Scripture that gives us a picture of creation entering a state of corruption is in Genesis 3:14-19. Here, God exposes and explains the curse to Adam and Eve and to the serpent (satan). Notice, I said God *exposes and explains* the curse, I did NOT say that God *pronounced and instituted the curse.* We won't explore that point in fact here, however, I will simply say that God is neither the author nor the enforcer of the curse.

In Genesis 3, verse 17 (Amplified Bible),

God tells Adam,

> "... the ground is [now] under a **curse <u>because of you</u>**..."

The "ground" does not only represent the agricultural aspects of creation. This term "ground" represents all of creation that God gave man dominion over through Adam, including: animals, vegetation, water, humans, natural elements, climate, atmospheric conditions, etc.

Think about it, even though tornadoes form in the clouds and twist and spin all across the sky, are they destroying the sun, moon and the stars? No! Tornadoes only cause destruction when they come into contact with what's on the ground. Tornadoes cause death and destruction when they drop out of the sky and touch down on the ground.

Remember, Genesis 3:17 tells us that the ground is cursed **because of man**. Adam and Eve's sin initiated a set of events that put all of creation in a painful labor from which it is still waiting to be delivered (Romans 8:22). The non-human parts of God's creation did not willingly make itself cursed and corrupted. Romans 8:20 tells us that creation was made **subject to vanity** *(was put in bondage or made to be a slave to corruption)*.

The good news is that God gave His creation *"hope"* that it could be set free from the corruption caused by Adam's sin. That hope is in Romans 8:19 and 21. We see in these two verses that when the sons of God operate in our authority and dominion, we bring into manifestation creation's freedom from the curse; the same freedom that we have received through Christ.

Romans 8:21-22 tells us that creation is waiting in both pain and hope, like that of a woman in labor waiting in pain for the hope of delivering her baby. If creation's hope is to be fulfilled, it needs our help.

So, the question is not: *When is God going to deliver creation from the painful labor of the curse caused by man's sin?* The answer to that question is: *God will not deliver creation.* Verse 19 of Romans 8 tells us that creation is waiting for *"...the manifestation of the **sons of God.**"*

In other words, until the sons of God manifest who we really are in the power and dominion God bestowed upon us when He created us, creation will continue to groan and travail like a woman in labor who desperately desires to be delivered from the pain.

BEHIND

THE

CURTAIN

THE TEMPERATURE

SPEAK TO THE WIND... IT SHALL OBEY!

When it comes to Kingdom authority and dominion over the weather, many Christians make it something so far out there. When in reality, we control our physical environments all the time. For example, no one thinks it's far out to install heating and cooling systems and thermostats to control the physical environments of our homes, churches, office buildings and cars.

Believers are suppose to operate like a ***thermostat-*** setting and controlling the "temperature" in the physical environment of planet earth. Let's think about "temperature" in terms of the atmospheric conditions and climate in your particular part of the world and how this thermostat principle can practically be applied to your authority over the weather.

Today's digital thermostats are designed to be programmable so that we can control the temperature and climate in our homes. For example: you can decide that you want the Monday through Friday climate in your home to be 75 degrees from 5am to 7am *(while the family is getting dressed for school and work)*; 78 degrees from 7am to 6pm *(to save energy while no one is home)*; and 68 degrees from 6pm to 5am *(because you like a cooler climate for sleeping)*. You can exercise even tighter control over the climate in your home by programming the thermostat with different settings for Saturday and Sunday. The thermostats are designed to keep the climate in your home at your desired level of comfort. You can literally give your thermostat the "authority" to control the climate in your home 24/7, year 'round.

Just like a digital thermostat, you have the authority to control the earth's climate. God has given Believers the authority to control the atmospheric conditions of the earth. When the natural elements begin to align in ways that can result in severe weather, you are authorized to use words of authority and dominion to set the wind and rain (and all the elements) in alignment with your desired comfort level.

Learning to use your faith to exercise your authority over the weather begins with climate control at the individual level of your home and the geographic location of you and your family members at any point in time- at school, at work, at church, at the movies, or on vacation. Beyond the point of our personal lives, the goal should be taking authority over the weather and protecting our neighborhoods, cities, counties, states, and nations.

The cover of this book is an image of a Believer who is uncomfortable with the climate in her immediate surroundings. She understands that the enemy is working to align the natural elements against her peace, comfort and safety. This Believer uses her authority to pull back the curtain of strong winds, pouring rain and lightning that the enemy has stirred up to hide the sunshine and pleasant breeze that are just on the other side of her bold faith to use her authority over the weather. Even though we don't see her speaking, the action of pulling back the curtain symbolizes her speaking to the wind. The sunny sky on the other side of the curtain validates that the wind did indeed obey her command.

The point of the cover is to provide a visual image of the power Believers have when we use our authority and power to program the thermostat and set the temperature of the climate and atmosphere around us.

This is precisely what Jesus did and He rebuked His disciples for waking Him up rather than using their authority to do it themselves (Matthew 8:23-27). Jesus wanted these men to understand that they have the same authority that He has over the wind and sea.

If you are still asking yourself, does man really have authority over the wind and sea? I want to say again, the answer is YES, we absolutely do! The world is waiting on the sons of God to manifest our authority from the smallest of matters to the greater level of authority over all of creation itself.

As we exercise our dominion in this area of weather, more of the image of Christ is manifested in us and through us from faith to faith and glory to glory (2 Corinthians 3:18; Romans 1:17). That manifested glory will help us reach unbelievers because they will be impressed with the God Who has children that not only have, but are able to demonstrate, real authority and power over the wicked powers behind the curtain of severe weather.

THE WEATHERLIES

What is satan's job? I ask that question because we blame God for so much. With the way many Believers talk about and respond to destruction and disaster, we might as well take satan out of the equation. Too many of us are speaking and acting as if God is causing all of these things to happen.

To walk in power and authority over the weather, one of the most important things we have to have knowledge and understanding about is that EVERYTHING natural has something spiritual behind it that will either influence for good or for evil. There is a whole lot that goes on behind the curtain.

Jesus rebuked the wind and commanded the sea to be at peace and to be still (Mark 4:39). When you study this story, you will find that Jesus' words were directed at more than the wind and the sea that could be seen with the natural eye. Jesus was also dispossessing a demonic spirit of its power to control the wind and the sea.

Recorded in Matthew chapter 8 is the story of two men whom Jesus delivered from demonic possession. When the demons came out of the men, they went and took possession of a herd of swine. The pigs apparently did not want to be the earth house for evil spirits, so the whole herd ran "violently" off a steep cliff into deep waters and drowned themselves.

To the natural eye, it simply looked like the pigs were too dumb to realize they were about to run off a cliff into deep water. However, Matthew's account of the story informs us that there was spiritual activity behind the curtain of what looked like hogs gone wild.

So, what spiritual activity is behind the curtain of severe weather? My answer to that is the **WEATHERLIES** are behind severe weather and weather-related disasters.

What are "weatherlies"? The weatherlies are a special forces unit of wicked spirits within the kingdom of darkness whose assignment is to influence the climate and natural elements to cause hurt, harm, danger, destruction and death. They operate in and from the spiritual realm.

I am sure you are asking yourself, where in the Bible is the term "weatherlies"? The term is not in the Bible. It is simply a name that helped me understand what God was revealing to me about these unauthorized wicked spirits that are behind severe weather events and disasters. My belief is that "weatherlies" is probably not the actual name of these demons. The actual name would probably be something that we could not pronounce. In short, weatherlies is just a name that provides an easy to understand identity for these demonic spirts.

When I first received the revelation of this special forces unit of wicked spirits, I spelled it in the singular…

"**weatherly.**" I would rebuke the "weatherly" or the "weatherlys" (plural) behind whatever storm was brewing in my area. As I was writing this book, my editor recommended that I change the plural spelling to **"WEATHERLIES"** so that we followed standard spelling rules. Then, I saw something in the name...

weather-LIES!

These wicked spirits have an assignment to weave a web of **LIES** by using the natural elements to deceive us into believing that nature is behind the weather when it causes death and destruction or that God is using nature to punish and teach.

We have come to believe that these events are acts of God or acts of nature. Neither is true. These severe weather events are acts of satan- the **prince of the power of the air** (Ephesians 2:2).

Another thing I have come to understand about the

weatherlies is how they work…I should say, I understand some of it. The weather events just keep getting bigger and stronger and more destructive. Part of the reason for this is that there is usually more than one wicked spirit (and often times, many) wicked spirits behind these storms.

After you have practiced using your faith over the weather for a while and have gotten some results, You can perform your own experiment to test what I just said. The next time the news station is broadcasting uninterrupted coverage of a severe weather event, pay close attention:

- First, notice how the atmospheric conditions begin lining up to create a specific weather event (tornado, hurricane, strong winds, flooding rains, etc).
- Next, take authority over the elements and start rebuking the wicked spirits behind them. What usually happens is the radar begins to show some slowing down or breaking up or movement in a different direction.

- Then, stop praying and step away from the TV for a while. When you come back, you will probably hear the weather man say something like, "This band of storms had begun to slow down and breakup, but it is starting to regroup and is picking up speed and strength and will move into our area sooner than we estimated."

What's happening? Depending on how much we have developed our faith in this area of dominion and power, we either weaken these wicked spirits, completely stop them or have no effect at all.

Don't be discouraged if you are new at this; just keep at it. If you stick with it, your authority as a born-again Believer over these wicked spirits will manifest and you will see them weaken in their strength and power to misuse the elements in your territory. Soon, you will be completely stopping the severe weather events in your area. Many times, I have seen the meteorologist look very confused as to why a particular band of storms just skip over my area or weaken to the point of just a rain shower.

So, now that we understand who the weatherlies are, let's take a look at what the weatherlies are doing behind the curtain.

Many times, the weatherlies that are on the scene stirring up the severe weather have to call for reinforcements. That's when you see the **"band"** of storms **"regrouping"** and picking up speed and strength. The reinforcements show up and **band together**. Now, you have a larger group of wicked spirits that are working together as a destructive force behind the weather.

We see from the Bible that this activity of wicked spirits calling for reinforcements actually happens. Two of the Gospels, Matthew 12:43-45 and Luke 11:24-26, record Jesus exposing the spiritual activity behind a man who is delivered and set free from 1 wicked spirit only to be brought back into bondage again by that one inviting 7 more spirits that are even more wicked than him, leaving the man in a worse state than when he was first set free. Scripture says,

> *⁴³ when the unclean spirit is gone out of a man, he walketh through dry places, seeking rest, and findeth none.*

> *⁴⁴ Then he saith, I will return into my house from whence I came out; and when he is come, he findeth it empty, swept, and garnished.*

> *⁴⁵ Then goeth he, and* **taketh with himself seven other spirits more wicked than himself***, and they enter in and dwell there: and the last state of that man is worse than the first. Even so shall it be also unto this wicked generation.*

Now, until you grow in faith in this area of your authority, you may have to bind and rebuke the wicked spirits again when you hear the weather man say that the storm is regrouping or that another band of storms is beginning to form. That's o.k. The point is for you to begin taking dominion over the natural elements and speaking with authority to rebuke the wickedness behind the severe weather event.

John 10:10 says, *"The thief cometh not, but for to steal, and to kill, and to destroy..."* Jesus replied that He came to give us life and life more abundantly.

Now, from that passage of Scripture alone we see that anytime there is some stealing, killing and destroying going on, satan is behind it- not God. Look at the words again: *"the thief **cometh NOT** but for to steal, and to kill, and to destroy."* In other words, the thief (satan) will not come... *does not even bother to show up on the scene...*

unless there is an opportunity for he and his entourage of demons to steal, kill and destroy.

So, why do we blame God for these severe weather events? We have gotten so far away from biblical truths and authority, that we even blame God for what satan is doing. Scripture plainly tells us that satan is the father of lies and he works to deceive the whole world.

The goal of this chapter is to expose the weatherlies and provide you with a look at the spiritual activity behind the curtain of tornadoes and other severe weather. Having knowledge of the enemy's tactics and strategies should help us to stop blaming God and do our part to protect our territory from the thief.

We have in so many ways allowed our adversary to do whatever he wants to do. But today is a new day; a new order is being established. I have declared war on the **WEATHERLIES**. I am inviting you to join me.

Let's study the Word, listen to the instructions of the Holy Spirit and practice using our authority as God's special forces unit and begin warring against the weatherlies, in Jesus' Name.

TERRITORIAL AUTHORITY

The book of Daniel provides us with clear evidence that the wicked forces of darkness have specified authority over particular territories. They have work roles that are assigned, and they have designated geographic territory where they fight to stop the will of God and the will of godly men in those territories.

Daniel 10:12-13, 20 (Contemporary English Version)
> *[12] Daniel, don't be afraid! God has listened to your prayers since the first day you humbly asked for understanding, and he has sent me here.*
> *[13] But the **guardian angel of Persia opposed me** for twenty-one days. Then Michael, who is one of the strongest guardian angels, came to rescue me from the **kings of Persia.** Then the angel said:*
> *[20] "...Soon I must leave to fight against the guardian angel of Persia. Then after I have defeated him, the **guardian angel of Greece** will attack me."*

SPEAK TO THE WIND... IT SHALL OBEY!

Daniel prayed and was waiting on God to answer him when after 21 days the angel of the Lord finally showed up. The angel told Daniel that God heard his prayer and sent the answer on the very first day that Daniel prayed, but a very strong demon with the title, "**prince of Persia**" **(singular)** started a battle with God's angel to stop the answer from reaching Daniel. This demon prince called in reinforcements that were stronger than him. It was more than one demon that came to help the demon prince because the Bible tells us that the reinforcements had the title, "**kings of Persia**" **(plural)**. The battle lasted 21 days. It was after Michael arrived (another of God's angels) and helped the messenger angel break free from the kings of Persia that God's answer to Daniel was finally delivered.

All power and authority and dominion is the Lord's and He has chosen to share it with us, His born-again children. Before sin, our authority was not challenged, but it is now. We have to fight to control the climate in our territory.

Matthew 11:12: *"And from the days of John the Baptist until now the Kingdom of Heaven suffereth violence, and the violent take it by force."*

The people in my sphere of influence expect me to take control of the natural elements. My wife and kids, parents, in-laws, church family, much of my extended family and even many friends and co-workers… they all just expect me to operate in my authority and command the weatherlies.

My faith in this area started small. For instance, when I needed it not to rain or I needed the rain to stop, I would command the rain to be still. It didn't take long at all for me to begin seeing results.

Then, I expanded the use of my authority to

decreeing that trees and power lines would not fall on my property to commanding wind gusts and dangerous lightening to cease. I was sort of like David: I slew the lion, then the bear, then the giant.

Now, it's just what I do. I operate in manifested authority over the natural elements. I give all the glory to God because this power is not about me. This is about God receiving glory when His children demonstrate tangible power to the world in His Name. This is about God saving lives through the dominion He gave to man. This is about God's love for people.

My authority allows me a range of territory. Exactly what that range is, I don't know. What I do know is that my parameter is protected.

Christmas day, 2016. My family is celebrating at my parent's home. My wife and kids are there, my brother and his daughter, my wife's mother and a married couple who are family friends. We are all Believers.

We were watching the football game and the local news station interrupted the broadcast with breaking news about the weather. The report was that a tornado had been spotted in the Jefferson County area and people should take cover and take safety precautions. I immediately got up and stepped outside. I didn't say anything, so some of the people there knew what I was about to do, some did not.

Once I was outside, I did what I normally do which is take my authority. I spoke to the winds from the north, south, east and west and commanded them to be at peace and to be still. Then, I released the Blood of Jesus over the atmosphere and over the area where we were and the surrounding areas and I loosed the angels to be released in the area. There was a small breeze blowing, but that had pretty much stopped by the time I finished praying. So, I went back inside of the house.

The weather coverage had ended, so the game was back on and I sat down and continued watching the game. Almost immediately, the lights went out. From inside of the house, we didn't see or hear the wind blowing, there was no thunder or lightening, but the lights went out.

Let me say something right here about authority: you cannot allow your faith to get sidetracked if you take a stand on your authority and then something comes along that makes it look like your authority is not working. The enemy wants to always make God's Word and God's people look foolish, powerless and ineffective. You have to know that you know, satan is a defeated foe. Back to the story…

So, the lights are out and we decide to go outside and see what was going on. Remember, we haven't heard even the slightest rumble of bad weather. When we open the door, the telephone pole and power lines across the street were on the ground. A half block to our right, houses were affected. Some had their roofs blown off or damaged and the church in that area had been affected. Other homes on nearby streets were affected, but absolutely nothing was affected at my parent's home, on their property nor at the homes and properties surrounding them.

Something else that is really remarkable was my mother's Christmas wreaths were not blown down or even blown out of place. The same wind that was powerful enough to knock down the telephone poll directly across the street, could not (had been stripped of the power to) even shift Christmas decorations on my parent's property.

It dawned on me much later how similar our Christmas day experience was to the children of Israel and the death angel passing over. All that chaos was going on in Egypt, but they had peace in the house and just kept eating the Passover lamb. When I came back in the house after praying, no one was reacting in fear. Everyone was still sitting in the same seat and we just continued to talk and fellowship.

Saying, I hope I'm protected; I hope I'm safe in this bathtub is not faith and they are not the words that back up your authority. By default, you are giving the enemy permission to steal, kill and destroy when you say I hope I'm safe in this bathtub.

BATHUB FAITH defines and restricts the territorial boundaries of your authority to the bathroom. Why not just believe that the storm will not come near your house (or whatever dwelling you're in at the time of the storm)? If you believe that God can protect you in the bathtub, why not believe that He can protect you and your whole house.

Our God-given authority is not just for sickness, unclean spirits, and diseases. We have authority to come against and subdue anything that is contrary to God's Word, but we will have to fight (doing spiritual warfare) to regain that territory and to keep that territory.

In Ephesians 6:12, we get another look behind the curtain and again we see rank (just like we saw the demonic prince and the demonic kings in the book of Daniel). Here we find an explanation of how the kingdom of darkness has structured its forces into different ranks and realms of influence:

1. principalities
2. powers
3. rulers of the darkness of the world
4. spiritual wickedness in high places

Ephesians 6:12

> *"For **we wrestle not against flesh and blood**, but against principalities, against powers, against the rulers of the darkness of this world, against spiritual wickedness in high places."*

The reference to **"flesh and blood"** is not just referencing the people factor in spiritual warfare. Flesh and blood is a reference to anything that we can see in the natural realm- *people, strong winds, dangerous lightening, roaring seas, shaking and shifting ground (earthquakes),* etc. The Word of God is exposing the work of evil spirits that is cloaked or hidden behind the behavior of people and the natural elements. However, we see here in Ephesians 6 that our warfare is not with the natural elements that we see in severe weather. Our warfare is with spiritual forces of darkness.

God has established rank for us in the Body of Christ. As we move up in rank, there is increased responsibility, authority, and power that come with it. What differentiates a deacon, a pastor, a bishop, and an apostle from one another? Increased responsibility, authority and power.

The angels are ranked and so are demonic forces. The kings of Persia showed up in the book of Daniel to help the prince of Persia stop God's messenger angel.

Michael, an angel with more rank and greater strength had to come and help the messenger angel break free from the demonic forces assigned to stop the will of God in that part of the earth. As we operate in more of our authority, we get more rank. God gives us more responsibility (larger territory to cover) and more power (increased ability to subdue more powerful weather events).

As I close this chapter on authority and territorial boundaries, I want to address a few issues. One question that I believe is really important to answer is:

How do we know what weather territory our authority covers?

The simple answer is as much territory as your faith can cover and get results. Simply put, if you have not developed your faith to stop the rain when you need it to stop, don't try to tackle a tornado. Go ahead and take safety precautions in the midst of a severe weather event while still exercising your authority. Command the wind to be at peace and to be still, then take whatever natural precautions you feel led to take. There is no shame in growing. Just keep practicing on non-life-threatening weather events until you see consistent results.

Another question that we need to answer is:

How do we know when the weather is just nature doing what nature does?

This answer is simple as well: **EVERYTIME** there is a **destructive** weather event, the weatherlies are behind it. Nondestructive weather events are just nature. This is nature just doing what nature does.

Like the body, when the spirit of man goes out of the body, no function takes place. Nature acts without destruction where there is no evil spirit force behind it.

As far as the territorial boundaries of my authority, I have this **UNIVERSAL REMOTE CONCEPT**: wherever I am, wherever my family is and wherever I have authority

SPEAK TO THE WIND… IT SHALL OBEY!

(like the area of town where my church is located), no matter the distance from me, I apply my authority! When nature begins to travail and groan… in whatever form- *tornado, earthquake, hurricane, flood, etc…* I have the authority over that so-called act of "nature" because there are weatherlies behind it with the goal of bringing destruction and harm to me and those people and places connected to me.

Take your authority over severe and dangerous weather because it is not nature nor is it God. There are weatherlies behind the curtain of EVERY severe weather event.

THE

KEYS

OF

AUTHORITY

THE POWER OF AGREEMENT

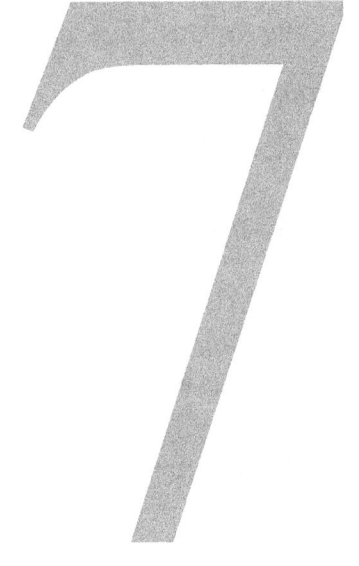

SPEAK TO THE WIND… IT SHALL OBEY!

There is great power in agreement. Throughout the Bible, both the Old and New Testament, Scripture informs us that agreement, unity, and harmony are very powerful forces in natural success and spiritual power. Agreement is an important key to activating our spiritual authority over the weather.

[19] Again I say unto you, That if two of you shall agree on earth as touching anything that they shall ask, it shall be done for them of my Father which is in heaven. [20] For where two or three are gathered together in my name, there am I in the midst of them.

Agreement is so powerful that Jesus, Himself told us whatsoever we ask in agreement, it SHALL BE DONE! There are at least 4 levels of agreement:

1. agreement with the Word of God
2. agreement with others (spouse, family, friends etc.)
3. agreement in the congregation
4. agreement in the Body of Christ (ultimate)

As it relates to your authority over the weather, the most important is agreement with the Word of God. Other people have no authority to stop your spiritual authority and dominion. So, while having agreement with other people about protection and safety is absolutely what we should seek, God only requires that *your heart, your faith* and *your words* agree with His Word to have Heaven backup your authority.

Matthew 16:19 says:

*"And I will give unto thee the **keys of the kingdom of heaven**: and whatsoever thou shalt **bind** on earth shall be bound in heaven: and whatsoever thou shalt **loose** on earth shall be loosed in heaven."*

What does **bind** mean? The Greek word is "**deo**" – it means to be in bonds, knit, tie, wind, to petition, to pray, to make request. So, based on this definition we are to:

- ✓ put the weatherlies in bonds
- ✓ knit them
- ✓ tie them
- ✓ wind them
- ✓ petition against them
- ✓ pray against them, and
- ✓ make a request against them.

When we FIRST do our part, Heaven will back us up.

Again, we are to operate like thermostats, not thermometers. With words that bind the weatherlies, we are to establish the climate on the earth, but we have been doing the opposite. When the weather man tells us that the atmospheric conditions are lining up to create some severe weather event, we begin speaking words and doing things that agree with the temperature the weather man is setting. We say things like, *"A tornado is going to hit our area tonight."* Then, we start watching the news non-stop, emptying the closets and putting blankets in the bathtub. Rather than "setting" the temperature with our words, we accept the thermometer's (i.e., weather radar's) temperature reading, then speak and act as if there is nothing we can do about it. What we should do is speak words that agree with the Word.

Let's look again at Matthew 16:19. If binding is one thing, what is loosing? The Greek word is **"luo"** – it means to break up, destroy, dissolve, melt, put off.

So, based on this definition, we are to:

- ✓ break up the tornado weatherlies
- ✓ destroy them
- ✓ dissolve them
- ✓ melt them
- ✓ put them off.

Are you getting this, yet? Are you getting fired up, yet? Are you ready to take back the wind and the rain for the Kingdom of Heaven?

Psalm 103:20 says that God's angels hearken unto the **voice** of the Word. In order for God's angels to work on your behalf, your VOICE has to speak God's Word.

God has given His angels charge over you (given them an assignment); to keep you in all of your ways (Psalm 91). However, they won't violate your word. If your words are not faith words that agree with God's Word, your angels have nothing to work with.

Remember, satan is a twister of what God has created and established. The forces of the kingdom of darkness (demonic angels) also have an assignment to respond to what we say out of our mouths or they function as outlaws manifesting their own will.

The final thing I want to say about agreement with the Word starts with a question. **Other than Jesus, has any other man commanded the natural elements?**

SPEAK TO THE WIND... IT SHALL OBEY!

Well, let's start with Jesus. Remember, Jesus did not operate in the earth as God. When He was born into the world, he operated as a born-again man... the last Adam. So, anything that we see Jesus do, any other born-again human can do. Also remember, Jesus rebuked His disciples for not using their own authority to rebuke the wind and the sea. He told them that there was no need to wake Him up when the boat began to fill with water. He was disappointed at how little faith they had.

Now, you could get in error and believe that the only reason the disciples would have been able to rebuke the wind and the sea is because they were with Jesus. You could get in error and believe they would not have had that power if Jesus wasn't with them, but that's not true. Scripture records another man using his authority to control the climate and direct the natural elements and Jesus was not physically with him when he did it.

2 Corinthians 13:1 says, "...*in the mouth of two or three witnesses shall every word be established.*"

So, all we need are two witnesses and right now we actually have **14 witnesses** that can testify that a man has authority over the elements: Jesus did it; the 12 disciples can testify that Jesus told them they could do it; and Elijah did it.

Elijah- the Tishbite, was a Prophet of God. We have a man in a physical body (so he is authorized by God to operate in dominion on the earth). I Kings 17: 1 and James 5:17 tells us that Elijah commanded the climates.

> *"And Elijah the Tishbite, who was of the inhabitants of Gilead, said unto Ahab, As the LORD God of Israel liveth, before whom I stand, there shall not be dew nor rain these years, but **according to my word**."*

Notice, Elijah did not say, *according to words from God's mouth;* he said, according to my (Elijah's) words. Elijah was talking to a king- someone who understands and operates in authority, dominion and power. Yet, Elijah did not back down in the face of natural authority. He spoke, the climate responded and Heaven backed him up.

Basically, what he said to king Ahab was something like this: *as long as God is alive, my words are backed up (enforced) by the authority He has given to me.*

The Book of James, chapter 5, is even more definitive about this man's authority over the climate:

[17] Elias [same guy, Elijah] was a man subject to like passions as we are, and he prayed earnestly that it might not rain: and it rained not on the earth by the space of three years and six months. [18] And he prayed again, and the heaven gave rain, and the earth brought forth her fruit.

SPEAK TO THE WIND... IT SHALL OBEY!

In the same way that Elijah did not lay down his authority in the face of natural authority, neither should we. The weather man, climate predicting technology like the weather radar, nor the roaring sights and sounds of the natural elements themselves... none of them... should have the final word. Our agreement with God's Word is the final word!

THE BELIEVERS
WEATHER FORECAST

What if the weather man (or woman) came on the air and did more than give us the facts of a potential severe weather event? What if he or she released words of faith instead of words of fear?

Well, for one thing, they would be ostracized. More times than not, you will be ostracized when you bring God into any secular profession. We can be fairly certain that we will not hear the meteorologist binding and loosing as he explains what's happening on the weather radar. So, how should we view the weather report? Your perspective about the authority of the weather report will either restrict your authority over the weather or it will give you the information you need to focus your faith and subdue the weather.

For the Believer, the role of the weather man should be the same as that of the doctor. The doctor does not have final say about the health of your body. As a Believer, you should see the doctor and his report as information, ONLY! When the doctor completes his examination and receives the results of the medical tests, if the diagnosis is that there is some **DIS-EASE** somewhere in your body, don't panic! All he has done for the Believer is given you information that you should use to focus your faith towards dispossessing that dis-ease of its power to operate in your body. The doctor and diagnosis do not have final say about the health of your body. After all, *"by Jesus' stripes you are [already] healed."*

The negative report just simply means that some part of your natural body is not at EASE and not at PEACE; but this is an unlawful state for the body of a born-again child of God. You have the right to command it to be repaired or replaced.

Thank God for the doctor's report that alerted you to the situation; you do NOT thank God for the sickness because He didn't give it to you. You are thankful because God gave medical science the wisdom that ALERTED you to the disorder in your body.

As Believers, it is God's report that we believe... about our health, wealth, relationships, and everything else. Well, it's the same for the weather man. His report should be taken simply as information that ALERTS us to the natural elements that wicked spirits are attempting to control.

Their game plan is to create negative weather events that have the potential to steal your peace, kill you if it could and destroy your property whenever possible. At the very least, the spiritual wickedness behind negative weather wants to steal your comfort and convenience by knocking out your electricity, bursting water mains so that you don't have running water for a while, and frustrate you because you don't have internet and cable.

For the Believer, the weather man's report should be viewed as information, ONLY! Use it to focus your faith towards dispossessing those wicked spirits of their power. With your God-given authority, you can stop them from using the natural elements to steal, kill and destroy. Take heed how you view the weather man and his report. Your perspective will impact your authority over the weather.

Now, let's sneak a peek and listen in on what a Believer's weather forecast might sound like.

The following is a newscast by a Meteorologist on a Christian television station that broadcasts godly programs, sports, entertainment and weather.

. . . .

```
We interrupt our regularly scheduled
    programming to bring you live
coverage of severe weather happening
       now in our viewing area
```

. . . .

Hello, I am Meteorologist, Bob Christian. We are coming to you live on **WCAN**- the **C**hristian **A**uthority **N**etwork.

At WCAN, we believe that Believers have authority over the weather. We are monitoring a weather pattern that looks like it is attempting to twist the natural elements of wind and rain in a way that creates a high probability of our area experiencing some severe weather.

We are alerting you to this weather pattern so that all of us Believers can get on one accord and take our authority over the spiritual wickedness behind these elements.

Believers, we know that God has given us total dominion over His creation, so let's use our authority to render ineffective this weather pattern and the spiritual wickedness behind it.

Meteorologist- Bob Christian, goes on to say to the television, radio and internet audience...

Call those Believers who are prayer warriors and who know they have authority over the weather and wicked spirits so that we can assist the natural elements. They need our help to respond like they were created to respond... as a blessing to us and not a curse.

Get in agreement with me and speak to the wind with authority and command it to obey you!

In Jesus' Name.

SPEAK TO THE WIND

SPEAK TO THE WIND... IT SHALL OBEY!

The most important thing you need to do as you operate in your authority over the weather is purposely listen for and follow the instructions of the Holy Spirit. **Whatever He tells you to do, do it!**

I really cannot give you a set of steps or a process because there is no substitute for the present help of the Lord right in the moment of your time of need. It really comes down to your faith in the authority you have over the weather and having a relationship with God where you can hear His instructions and do and say what He tells you to be protected. However, there are guiding principles in the Word of which we should have knowledge and be prepared to execute.

GUIDING PRINCIPLES FOR SPEAKING TO THE WIND

- Take Authority over the natural elements
- Bind the activity of the natural elements
- Take Authority over the wicked spirits
- Bind the activity of wicked spirits
- Loose the angels of God to stop the enemy and protect people, property and possessions
- Release the Blood of Jesus over people and territory
- Pronounce decrees and make declarations that agree with the Word of God and your faith confessions
- Watch your words. Speak only those words that agree with what you have decreed. Speak words of faith, ONLY!

Decree this Prayer

Every time you hear a report that the weather is about to become severe, stretch your hands toward the TV or radio and say this:

Father, in the Name of Jesus, I take authority over the winds and the atmosphere. I bind every tornadic activity (severe weather activity) and its intent to function and I command it to cease in Jesus' Name. I take authority over every wicked spirit and I bind them in the Name of Jesus and I command them to be at peace and to be still. I loose the angels of God and release my ministering angels to go forth and fight on my behalf according to Psalm 103:20 to stop, veto, annihilate and destroy any intent of satan and his host. I release the Blood of Jesus over my home and every dwelling place that I and my family occupy. I release the Blood of Jesus over the surrounding areas. I decree and declare that no damage, no trees, no power of demonic activity shall come near my dwelling according to Psalm 91. I now decree peace by the Name that is above every name. And I have what I say now, **in Jesus' Name! Amen.**

Take Authority Over The Natural Elements

Say, "North winds, south winds, east winds and west winds, I am speaking to you from my God-given position of authority and dominion over you. In the Name of Jesus, I command you to cease your destructive operation NOW!"

Take Authority Over Wicked Spirits

Say, "Spiritual wickedness behind the disorderly conduct of the wind and rain. In the Name of Jesus, I bind you and dispossess you of your power. You are stripped of your power to operate through the natural elements. Wicked spirits, I command you to be at PEACE and to BE STILL NOW, in Jesus' Name!"

STATISTICS

I am saying a lot in this book, but really- is it that serious? April 25-28, 2011 was called **tornado outbreak**. Why?

55 tornadoes hit the state of Alabama on April 27, 2011 alone. There was a total of 173 tornadoes on April 27- a new one-day record. There was a total of 326 confirmed tornadoes over the April 25-28 outbreak.

238 **DEAD**; 340 across all states, 2219 **INJURED**.

6237 homes, 1275 mobile homes and 295 apartment units **DESTROYED**.

5039 homes, 615 mobile homes and 163 apartment units **SEVERELY DAMAGED**.

4613 homes, mobile homes and apartments damaged but mostly habitable. 4824 homes, mobile homes and apartments with minor damage, broken windows etc. 654 families displaced from public or government assisted housing units. 1500 people in 65 Red Cross shelters.

42 Alabama counties declared federal disaster areas.

2.6 – 4.2 billion insurance claims expected.

3055 unemployment filings.

Up to 600,000 people without power, as Browns Ferry Nuclear Power Plant went offline.

All of this is just from a few days of satanic work. Yet, we have chosen to label this an act of God. If these things are acts of God, why are we praying? Let's keep our mouths shut and let God do His work. These things are not God's doing; it is satan! I hate even making reference to his name in this book.

John 10:10 separates the two kingdoms and defines their nature. Jesus said, *"The thief cometh not but for to steal, and to kill and to destroy."* Then, He informed us of His part: *"I am come that they might have life and that they might have it more abundantly."*

Using just this verse alone, how can you not see this kind of death and destruction as an act of satan? God has nothing to do with it.

Jeremiah 29:11 says, *"For I know the thoughts that I think toward you, saith the LORD, thoughts of peace, and not of evil, to give you an expected end."*

Really, God does not need me to defend His character, but there is someone out there who is looking for the truth. And, the truth is: severe weather and weather-related disasters are not acts of God. There are wicked spirits that use the natural elements to steal, kill and destroy. I believe so many more people can be protected and kept safe if Believers would just begin to operate in our authority over dangerous weather and the wicked spirits behind it.

My prayer is that the revelation and information in this book has inspired and motivated you to join me in learning and growing in this area of our God-given dominion and authority. We can indeed

SPEAK TO THE WIND...

IT SHALL OBEY!

ABOUT THE AUTHOR

PASTOR RENARD FARRIOR is the Senior Pastor of International Faith Ministries, a non-denominational church located in Tarrant, Alabama- *(a community in the Birmingham-Metro area).*

Pastor Farrior is married to Sonya who serves with her husband in the ministry. The couple has two sons- Renard Jr. and Reshad.

Pastor Farrior was called by God in the year 2000 to "bring freedom to the nations." With his first published book, "Speak To The Wind… It Shall Obey!" Pastor Farrior believes he has taken another giant step in fulfilling that call.

www.ingramcontent.com/pod-product-compliance
Lightning Source LLC
LaVergne TN
LVHW051505070426
835507LV00022B/2944